Be Healed and Stay Healed In

Jesus Name

(A Book of Testimonies)

By

ALETHA RENA DOGGETT

Be Healed and Stay Healed in Jesus Name
By Aletha Rena Doggett: Owner and Author
Copyright © 2011 by Aletha Rena Doggett
Revised March 2024
ISBN-13: 978-1477402467 (Paperback)

ARD Book Services, LLC
A Christian Publishing Consultant
United States of America
www.ardbookservices.com

DEDICATION

This book is dedicated to the body of Christ. My hope and prayer is that you will be healed in God's way and not by the ways of the world. Throughout the Bible, you never heard of Jesus or any of the disciples taking sick folk to a doctor or physician. Although Luke was a physician you still never heard of any account after Jesus was born that the sick were taken to any doctor. Jesus healed all manner of sickness, and He is expecting us to do the same. I hope that you believe in God for divine healing and resist sickness until the end. God the Father who art in Heaven and His only begotten Son, Jesus my Lord and Savior, and the Holy Spirit should receive all the Glory for healing. The Holy Spirit taught me how to overcome sickness and diseases and he will teach you how to do the same.

ACKNOWLEGEMENTS

I would like to first thank my Heavenly Father for giving me the gift to express my faith by way of publishing and writing books. I would like to thank the Lord for salvation and for baptizing me in the Holy Ghost in 1989 at Greater Grace Temple, in Detroit, Michigan. I would like to thank my sisters Sharon and Sylvia for helping me edit my book, my uncles, aunts, and cousins (the Evans Family) for being supportive of me. I would like to also thank my Pastors from down through the years: Bishop David L. Ellis, Apostle John Eckhardt, Reverend Gwen Hudson Tate, and Pastor Bill S. Winston. I would like to also acknowledge and thank my new friends and church family at Jesus People Life Changing Ministries with Pastor and Prophetess Mingo.

TABLE OF CONTENTS

INTRODUCTION

Dear Friends,

Before we get started you must know these certain truths:

1. First of all, God desires to heal you and make you whole.

2. Even though God allowed physicians to walk the earth, God Almighty never depended on any man to assist him regarding healing. God is the great physician all by Himself.

3. Asa was a king and sought God for many things. When it was time for Asa to go to war, he consulted God for protection. When it was time for Asa to find shelter and food for his family, he consulted God for provision. But when it was time for Asa to consult God for a healing in his feet, he consulted not God but instead, he consulted the physicians. God became very angry with Asa and allowed no man to heal him, and he died with the disease in his feet (2 Chron 16:12).

4. Therefore, this is why God gave us (the body of Christ) the GIFTS of healing. I learned that God has many gifts to heal many different situations. This book can be used to heal your physical, spiritual, emotional, or mental situation as long as you seek God. The key is that we must work God's word to see results. This means meditating, confessing, believing, speaking, and writing God's word.

5. Jesus always raised the multitudes from the dead. Even when family members thought their sons and daughters had died – Jesus said they were only sleeping because there was life still left in them.

6. Dorcas (Talitha) was a woman of good works and when she died, according to the book of Acts, one of the disciples raised her from the dead and she continued to live a long life. I was shocked when I read that Dorcas had been raised from the dead.

7. No matter how bad you feel never trust in your feelings. The devil is a liar and operates in the sense realm. This is why we must never agree with sickness or death. Instead always

confess, "I believe I receive my healing in Jesus' name."

8. Trust in the Word of God and stand on the side of the Cross. Believe what Jesus said, "By His stripes, we are healed."

9. Last but not least, you can live as long as you desire in God's will – the choice is up to you. As long as you abide in God, he will abide in you. God promises us Eternal Life and says if you honor your father and mother in the Lord, you shall receive long life (Ephesians 6:1-8).

Now that you have an understanding of God's truth; be Healed, Stay Healed, and Know that you are Healed, In Jesus' Name. May God Bless you and I will keep you in my Prayers!

Aletha R. Doggett

HOW TO USE THIS BOOK

*T*he following chapters will be filled with revelations and testimonies that have inspired me since the early years of my walk with the Holy Spirit. After you read the chapters on my testimonies you will be given over 25 healing scriptures to read, meditate, mutter, and write. Each scripture will be written several times on a page for you to speak out loud, meditate on, and write out. It is your job to read, repeat, and write the scripture to build your faith. Your goal is to continue this process until the word is sown into your heart. This exercise is an example of how a farmer grows his crops. He plants the seed into good ground, then he waters it and watches his crop grow. Only in this example, the word of God is the seed, you are the Sower, and your heart is the good ground. Take your daily bread each day which is the word of God and follow these simple instructions for your continual healing. After you receive the word of life through God's divine scriptures you will receive some amazing impartation. Be Blessed in Jesus' name. All Scriptures are taken from the KJV Bible only.

CHAPTER 1

DELIVERED FROM LAXATIVES
&
CONSTIPATION

When I was 26 years old I had a very hard time having a bowel movement. I was constipated all the time. I thought I had a serious colon problem and that I would eventually undergo a serious medical procedure. I started visiting the doctor to find out what my problem was, and he put me on a medication called Perdiem. Perdiem was an over-the-counter natural laxative, with high grams of fiber. It was a very bad-tasting laxative, and it looked like small little granules that I would have to scoop up with a spoon. It was horrible trying to digest and swallow that big spoonful of laxative three times a day.

SIDE EFFECTS

I followed that routine for about a week and the laxative worked after the first day. However, the Perdiem was so strong that when it began to take effect in my body I would break out in sweat and my stomach would start to cramp. The Perdiem was working through my upper and lower colon breaking up food that had been stored in my colon walls for weeks.

I eliminated what seemed like pounds of waste in one day. But when the process was all over, I was clean as a whistle. My stomach was flat and no longer bloated. I would look into the toilet to see the disgusting waste that came out of my body and would praise the Lord. I was shocked that my stomach could hold so much garbage. I lost 10 pounds during this cleansing process.

The Doctor told me that most people have a bowel movement after every meal or at least once a day. Well, for me to have a bowel movement once a week was a challenge. I would try to use the bathroom day after day but not until after about day number 4 or 5 did I have a release. When I finally had a bowel movement it was very hard getting the stool out of my system. I would be in the bathroom doing acrobats on the toilet trying to push the stool out of my body. It was a wrestling match. I would have to pray to get through a bowel movement successfully.

REVELATION

I began to take a different kind of laxative because the Perdiem was way too strong. I found myself taking the chocolate laxative instead, something more on the light side and that did not taste so bad. I was still having problems having a bowel movement and by this time I would go up to a week at a time without one. So, I began to take the chocolate laxative twice a month, giving me 2 good laxatives every couple of weeks. I knew that taking too many laxatives was not good for the body and could cause greater damage than if I had not taken any laxatives at all. But in my mind, I thought taking one laxative every couple of weeks was not so bad.

TESTIMONY – THE LORD IS A DELIVERER

Well, one day I went into my kitchen and opened the cabinet to take more chocolate laxatives. I figured since it had been a while since my last bowel movement, I would increase the dosage. I thought by doing so, that the laxative would have more of an impact on my colon, and would allow me to have more of a bowel movement in a quicker amount of time. Well, the Lord said NOT SO.

The Lord knew that I had opened up a door to something very dangerous but allowed my spiritual eyes to open. While I was standing in my kitchen holding the laxatives in my hand the Lord spoke to me very clearly and said, "Look at what you are doing." I looked at the laxatives in my hand and all of a sudden, my eyes began to leave the earth realm and entered into the spiritual realm. I saw a spirit of suicide. Now mind you, before the Lord opened my eyes, I saw nothing more than a few innocent laxatives in my hand that were going to help me have another bowel movement, but the Lord knows best. When the Lord spoke to me and said, "Look at what you are doing," I began to realize the compassion Jesus had toward this situation. I immediately repented and asked the Lord to forgive me and help me.

GOD'S PLAN TO HELP ME ESCAPE

Shortly after the Lord gave me the revelation about the laxatives, God gave me my escape. Always remember when the Lord speaks to you about a situation, he has a plan for your deliverance in mind. The very next day I was on the elevator leaving my apartment in downtown Chicago when all of a sudden, I heard two old white women in their late 70s talking about grocery shopping. Well, it wasn't that I was ease-dropping or anything like that, but the Lord allowed me to overhear what the women were talking about. All of a sudden, the Holy Spirit allowed me to hear one woman say, "POST RAISIN BRAN CEREAL HAS 9 GRAMS OF FIBER AND IS GREAT FOR CONSTIPATION." When I heard those words, I knew the Lord was speaking to me. The chains of laxatives instantly broke off my mind. I immediately took that word of wisdom, went to the grocery store, and bought up a few boxes of Post Raisin Bran Cereal, and have been saved ever since that day. I am enjoying having a daily bowel movement because I now include Post Raisin Bran cereal in my diet.

Just when the devil was trying to destroy my colon with over-the-counter laxatives the Lord took me back to natural grains and fruits rolled up in a box of cereal! My colon is completely healed, and I have not taken over-the-counter laxatives in over 15 years.

NOTE: Let me say this also, the more laxatives you take the harder it becomes to release a natural bowel movement on your own. The consequence is that a person who takes frequent laxatives will eventually have to depend on stimulates to help push out their stool because the lower colon muscles would have become weak and lazy. Get in the habit of eating fruits and vegetables and believe in God for your healing the natural way. Stop taking those over-the-counter laxatives in Jesus' Name – they are not good for you!

CHAPTER 2

DELIVERED FROM TYLENOLS
&
MENSTRUAL CRAMPS

ACCEPTANCE

I suffered severe menstrual cramps for years before receiving the revelation about divine healing. I would have headaches, back pains, severe side cramps, and heavy bleeding that would cause me to have to use twice the amount of sanitary napkins each month. Year after year month after month I encountered menstrual distress. I thought the pains associated with a monthly menstrual cycle were a normal part of life, and that I had to accept every ache and pain associated with it. Not until the Lord began to speak to me about divine healing did, I realize the truth about divine health.

ROUTINE

Every month I would begin my 7-day menstrual cycle by taking Tylenol pills from sunup to sundown trying to find a way to subdue the menstrual cramps. I was taking anywhere between 8-12 Tylenol pills every month to help me get through my agonizing menstrual cycle. In my mind, I thought the Tylenol would help get rid of the pain and help me to sleep better, and for years the devil had my mind thinking that household medicines were the way to go. But the Lord began to teach me that the Word of God is my medicine. It seemed like the more I would take the Tylenol medicine the heavier my bleeding would become and the longer my cramps would last.

One day I woke up and began to take dominion over the Tylenol bottle. I said, Lord, I want to believe you to take away these menstrual cramps and take me off of this over-the-counter medication. I told the Lord that I do not believe it is your will for me to have to run to the drugstore every month to buy a bottle of pills to help me with my monthly menstrual cycle. So, I begin to trust God.

DELIVERED FROM TYLENOL

The first time I decided not to take the Tylenol medication to help me during my menstrual cycle my body went into total shock. However, I was determined to believe in God for my healing and vowed to myself that I was going to be Tylenol-free and cramps-free in Jesus' name. It took about 3 months of faith to believe that Tylenol was not my healer, but God was my healer. Sure enough, after about the 4th month, I begin to notice a change in my body. My bleeding was very light, I no longer had severe headaches, and the cramps were barely noticeable. After the 5th month, I was completely healed from Tylenol withdrawals and my body was operating on a normal rhythm free from monthly medication. I no longer have severe back pains, no more headaches, my bleeding is normal spotting, and I am using fewer sanitary napkins. The menstrual cramps have been completely healed in Jesus name and I look forward to my monthly menstrual cycle every month.

CHAPTER 3

DELIVERED FROM FLU SHOTS
&
MYSTERIOUS COUGHS

WE WALK BY FAITH

*E*very year around November I would begin to have flu-like symptoms and would confess that I was catching a cold. I would go through the normal routine of buying cold medicines and taking antibiotics to help get rid of the flu-like symptoms. Well, in 2004, my mind was renewed, and I stepped out on faith to believe that God would take these old habits away from me. I was tired of taking cold medicine and flu shots every year to help patch up a bad cold. By this time in my life, I concluded that all colds, flu, and sickness were demonic because I had read in the Word of God that Jesus healed all manner of sickness and disease. The Lord had already healed me of taking laxatives due to wrong eating patterns and healed my menstrual cramps. Why couldn't God heal me of a common cold or flu that millions of people confess to catching each year?

TAKE AUTHORITY

However, this one particular year I was not claim-
ing any more colds or flu. Although I still had flu-
like symptoms, I was not going to admit out of my
mouth that I had the flu. I was going to walk out on
faith and tell my body that by Jesus' stripes I am
healed. I would repeatedly tell my body "I am not
catching your cold because it's not mine any
longer." I confessed to myself that "I was not going
to take another pill, nor another spoon of cough
syrup because by Jesus' stripes I am healed." "I am
going to walk by faith!" After that season of taking
authority over the flu and common cold, I can admit
to you today that I have not had a cold since 2004.
God has completely healed me of the common
cold. I have not taken the flu shot nor have I taken
any over-the-counter cough medicine or any other
pharmaceutical drug since 2004. Jesus healed me
from cold medicines and flu shots. I am healed in
Jesus' name. Remember what the Bible says,
"Death and Life are in the power of the tongue and
those who love it will it the fruit thereof." Proverbs
18:22.

REVELATION

During this experience of winging off of flu shots and cold medicines, I realized that the more medication you take the longer it takes for your body to heal and cleanse. When I decided to replace the cold medicine, or the flu shot with a hot bowl of homemade chicken noodle soup and drank plenty of water with lemons my body felt at ease, and sleep to rest came more easily. I found that when my body was not filled up with antibiotics or cold medicines "the cold or flu" did not last as long in my body.

HOME REMEDY

Homemade Chicken noodle soup cooked with a lot of celery and drinking lots of water with lemon, and your favorite healing scripture will cleanse you quicker than most of these over-the-counter medicines. God never intended for us to pollute our bodies with pharmaceutical medication. However, under unusual circumstances, you may have to take certain medicines when you do just ask the Lord to bless it.

God delivered me completely from all over-the-counter medications, cold medicines, Tylenol, laxatives, and flu shots all in a matter of 2 years.

CASTING OUT DEVILS

I remember one day in 2001 a co-worker who was a man had been trying to befriend me. He was a weird individual and at the time I believed he was involved in sorcery and other dark magic because he would have all kinds of weird trinkets on his desk. I never confronted him about his weird behavior, but he would always come to my desk and say weird things. So then one week, I began to feel very sick and had an uncontrollable cough that I could not get rid of. So, I began to pray and ask God why was this cough still lingering on for weeks and why was this cough so harsh?

At the time, I was very active with my relationship with the Holy Spirit and was very prayed up at this time in my life. After a while, I knew that this cough was not associated with the common cold, but that it was demonic. So, I prayed and fasted and asked the Lord, "What is this cough and how do I get rid of it?" So, then the Lord spoke to me and said, "This is trickery sent by your co-worker, cast it out in my name." Therefore, I began to take authority over this devil and began casting it out. The Lord also began to open my eyes to where this man had been placing demonic trinkets all around my desk area at work and under my keyboard. I would look under my keyboard and say, "Why is this piece of metal under my keyboard?" Or I would begin noticing little things that were appearing out of place.

All during this time I was reading a Christian book by Rebecca Brown, "He Came to Set the Captives Free" and sure enough these same tactics that this man was using against me on the job were exposed in her very books. There was a page in her book that showed when warlocks and sorcerers try to put spells on you, they use small pieces of hidden medals, and place them in areas that are unknown to you – under a flowerpot, under a desk chair, etc. God revealed every one of his tactics to me and this person was amazed that I was finding all his schemes. God continued to bless me and kept me safe and drove that spirit right out of my chest in Jesus' name. The cough was cast out and I was protected in Jesus name.

So, therefore, God will heal you with his WORD and through Casting OUT in his Name. The Lord says that by his stripes we are healed, so, therefore, believe God and be healed.

One last note as I conclude this chapter: If you need to take your prescription medicine, just pray over it and ask God to curse all side effects. The examples that I share in this book was for individuals based on their own set of circumstances. Please use your own judgement and pray to God about everything. The Almighty God is the only Physician and He wants to get the glory out of healing your body. Do what he tells you to do, and you will stay healed. I can honestly say that so far I have been delivered from taking all prescription medications since 2004.

CHAPTER 4

GOD HEALED MY FORMER BOSS FROM BREAST CANCER

I remember back in 2003, my former Boss, Judith, weighed over 300 pounds and was diagnosed with breast cancer. Judith was always very outgoing and friendly around the office but when she heard about the news of her sickness, she became upset. Judith was told that she had two options: 1) To either take the radiation to burn out the cancer or 2) to change her lifestyle including diet and daily exercise. Judith immediately took action and chose option # 2. Judith decided that she would beat this sickness by eliminating certain foods from her diet.

A NEW DIET

The very first month Judith lost 30 pounds after she decided to no longer eat meats, white bread, dairy products, and soda pops. Judith then decided to take a cooking class to learn how to eat and prepare her food more properly. Judith's diet went from fried chicken and collard greens to fruits, salads, fresh

vegetables, and an occasional fish. Judith eliminated soft drinks, fruit juices, teas, and coffee from
her diet and drank an entire gallon of water each
day. Judith brought her lunch to work and never
swayed from her new diet. After about 6-8 months
Judith lost over 100 pounds and became free of
breast cancer. Judith was completely healed in Jesus' name!

GOD HEALS EVEN DOCTORS

Rebecca was a medical doctor who specialized in
oncology, the treatment of cancer patients. Rebecca
observed throughout her career that the patients
who were subjected to radiation did very poorly after their treatment. Even though Rebecca was
caught up in the world of medicine she had to offer
the radiation to her patients despite some of the neg-
ative side effects. Rebecca was very knowledgeable
in her profession and served on many medical
boards, spoke on a local radio station, and had
written many articles and magazines. Rebecca was
considered a very successful doctor in the eyes of
the medical world until she was diagnosed with the
same fate she saw in her patients.

TOOK A TURN FOR THE WORSE

Rebecca began to take a turn for the worse. She noticed a lump on her chest that eventually grew to the size of a grapefruit. Rebecca feared that she had breast cancer and prepared herself mentally as to how she would handle her condition. Once the sickness was confirmed, her colleagues immediately recommended that she start radiation treatments. Rebecca knew what radiation would do to the body, so her options were very slim. She ruled out radiation totally, but her colleagues began to ridicule her and call her crazy.

WEIGHT LOSS

Rebecca was already a tiny woman so losing over 60 pounds in a matter of months made her look very sickly and malnutrition. Rebecca was looking for a way out. Rebecca admitted that she had tried several different religions in the past but this time she wanted to know who could heal her of this disease. Rebecca tried Eastern Religion, Buddhism, and Islam, but none of these gods could help Rebecca. Until one day Rebecca got on her knees and called upon the name of the Lord of the Bible – Jehovah Rapha – The Almighty God.

COME BACK TO JESUS

Rebecca said one night she was in her bedroom and began to call upon the true and living God, and the Lord Jesus spoke to her. The Lord spoke to Rebecca and said remember the Levitical Laws found in the book of Leviticus. Rebecca said that the Holy Spirit began to minister to her about the foods she should eat and the food she should not eat. After about 6 weeks into the diet, Rebecca began to see a drastic change in the lump that was in her breast. It went from the size of a grapefruit to the size of a golf ball. After about 3 months or so, Rebecca was completely healed. The Lord healed Rebecca and gave her a new body! God gave Rebecca life through the Word of God and a new diet.

CHAPTER 5

POWERFUL FOODS FROM THE BIBLE
&
FOODS THAT I ATE GROWING UP

POMEGRANATE

I would like to first share with you my experience with how our Heavenly Father taught me which foods were good to eat and which foods were not good to eat. Even from a young child the LORD GOD was my teacher.

I remember the very first fruit God introduced me to be the pomegranate fruit. You know the big, hard, red, seedy, juicy fruit that is filled with nutrients and goodness.

Well, the pomegranate was given to me for the first time one day on my way home from elementary school. I must have been about 9 years old when I was handed this big red fruit. While walking home, I sensed in my spirit that God was shining on me and that this piece of fruit was just not some ordinary fruit, but this was a piece of fruit called from heaven. Neither my parents nor my neighbors ever had a pomegranate in their home, so I felt special. My family basically ate apples, oranges, and an occasional pear. All I can remember saying is that God is shining on me because He just handed me a piece of fruit from the Bible. Here is a great definition:

[1]Pomegranate and its distinctive ruby-red jewel-like seeds have been used for medicinal purposes for thousands of years. The Middle Eastern fruit is claimed to be effective against heart disease, high blood pressure, inflammation, and some cancers, including prostate cancer. Pomegranate is a good source of fiber. The pomegranate has Anti-aging effects, Kidney protection, Liver protection and regeneration, Immune-boosting, Anti-allergic, Prostate-cancer protection, Breast-cancer protection, Skin-cancer protection, and Blood pressure normalizing. I recommend drinking pomegranate juice at least once a week.

FIGS

The fig was introduced to me when I was in my youth and was known as my favorite fruit-filled cookie. I loved the Fig Newton. Growing up in Detroit, Michigan I remember enjoying the fig Newton and at the time, when this cookie was introduced to me, I knew by the Spirit of the Lord, even at a young age, that the fig was a biblical fruit. I did not know that the fig and prune were similar and had dietary value. Later in life, I discovered that the fig was high in fiber.

The fig is a fruit mentioned in the Bible several times and the fig is also commonly known for how when Jesus cursed the Fig tree. Although dried figs are available throughout the year, there is nothing like the unique taste and texture of fresh figs.

[2]Figs are lusciously sweet with a texture that combines the chewiness of their flesh, the smoothness of their skin, and the crunchiness of their seeds. California figs are available from June through September; some European varieties are available through fall. Figs grow on the Ficus tree (Ficus carica), which is a member of the Mulberry family.

They are unique in that they have an opening, called the "ostiole" or "eye," which is not connected to the tree, but helps the fruit's development by increasing its communication with the environment. Figs range dramatically in color and subtly in texture depending upon the variety. The majority of figs are dried, either by exposure to sunlight or through an artificial process, creating a sweet and nutritious dried fruit that can be enjoyed throughout the year. Figs are high in Fiber, Vitamin B6, copper, Manganese, potassium, and pantothenic acid."

LEMONS

Lemons are an excellent source of vitamin C and are used for so many things. I first started using lemons as a cleanser to help purge my body from old toxins and later found out that lemons are used as a good laxative. I started using lemons to keep my breath, tongue, and pallet clean from leftover foods and started rubbing lemons on my hands after a meal. Lemons are a great deodorizer and are considered the third super food after sweet potatoes and tomatoes. Lemons are also good for hydrating your body by adding lemons to your water. Most people think that drinking a lot of water by itself will help hydrate your body, but it's the acidity of the lemons that helps with your hydration. So always add something acidic such as lemons or limes to your water if you need to hydrate yourself. Water by itself will not always do it. You should always add a little lemon to your water.

I remember one time I was riding the CTA bus in Chicago and a man was sitting in front of me who was telling a story about how he was President Kennedy's cook in the 60s. He said that one day the President wanted a steak as soon as possible and the only steak that was available was frozen. The cook pulled out a frozen steak and squeezed lemon juice over top of the steak to help unthaw the steak. He said the lemon would help melt the ice on the steak in seconds. I had learned from the man sitting in front of me on the bus that lemons can be used to thaw out frozen meat. Look at God. He always sends a little bird to teach us things if we just listen. So now I use lemons all the time! I use lemons to help with my digestion, as a liver cleanser, a breath deodorizer, a natural bathroom flush, and in most of my cooking!

OLIVES

Olives are one of my favorite fruits and were one of those items God showed me at a very young age. The Olive is surely a biblical fruit and is mentioned quite often in the Bible Book Zechariah Chapter 4. The green olive tree in this chapter of the Bible represents God's goodness, richness, maturity, health, nutrients, prominence, influence, full color, and most importantly the anointing. I love the green olives. The green olive was used extensively in the Bible as a sign of refuge and strength as well as a symbolic sign for the anointing oil. Full-grown olive trees and olive branches are mentioned several times in the book of Zechariah Chapter 4. God spoke to me and said read Zechariah Chapter 4 out loud.

ZECHARIAH CHAPTER 4

1 And the angel that talked with me came again, and waked me, as a man that is wakened out of his sleep.

2 And said unto me, What seest thou? And I said, I have looked, and behold a candlestick all of gold, with a bowl upon the top of it, and his seven lamps thereon, and seven pipes to the seven lamps, which are upon the top thereof:

*3 **And two olive trees by it, one upon the right side of the bowl, and the other upon the left side thereof.***

4 So I answered and spake to the angel that talked with me, saying, What are these, my lord?

5 Then the angel that talked with me answered and said unto me, Knowest thou not what these be? And I said, No, my lord.

6 Then he answered and spake unto me, saying, This is the word of the Lord unto Zerubbabel, saying, Not by might, nor by power, but by my spirit, saith the Lord of hosts.

7 Who art thou, O great mountain? before Zerubbabel thou shalt become a plain: and he shall bring forth the headstone thereof with shouting's, crying, Grace, grace unto it.

8 Moreover the word of the Lord came unto me, saying,

9 The hands of Zerubbabel have laid the foundation of this house; his hands shall also finish it; and thou shalt know that the Lord of hosts hath sent me unto you.

10 For who hath despised the day of small things? for they shall rejoice and shall see the plummet in the hand of Zerubbabel with those seven; they are the eyes of the Lord, which run to and fro through the whole earth.

11 Then answered I, and said unto him, What are these two olive trees upon the right side of the candlestick and the left side thereof?

12 And I answered again, and said unto him, ***What be these two olive branches which through the two golden pipes empty the golden oil out of themselves?***

13 And he answered me and said, Knowest thou not what these be? And I said, No, my lord.

14 Then said he, These are the two anointed ones, that stand by the Lord of the whole earth.

HONEY

Honey is used for so many different things such as weight loss, colds and coughs, healthier hair and skin, and the list goes on and on. I remember when my spiritual leader Reverend Gwen Hudson Tate introduced me to lemon water with honey, milk and honey, and hyssop, boy my life was so different. The Bible explains it best:

- My Son eat thou honey because it is good: Proverbs 24:13.
- Honey will help you discern the difference between good and evil when eaten in moderation: Isaiah 7:14.
- David the king gave his people honey, and butter to eat: 2 Samuel 17:29.
- He made him to such honey out of the rock: Deuteronomy 32:13.
- John the Baptist ate honey: Matthew 3:4.
- God created brooks of honey and butter: Job 20:17.

- Canaan is a land flowing with milk and honey: Exodus 3:8.
- Samson ate wild honey found in the carcass of a lion: Judges 14: 8-18.

HYSSOP

The Bible declares in Psalms 51, "Purge me with hyssop and I shall be clean wash me and I will be made whiter than snow. My friends, the hyssop tea is powerful. If you really want a clean temple and truly start a consecration before the Lord, I recommend Alvita Hyssop Tea Bags. This tea is 100% hyssop tea and if used regularly you will see a harmonious change take place in your spirit, soul, mind, and body.

This tea will cleanse you from the crown of your head to the soul of your feet. It will dismiss any foul odor you may have in your system, but it is not a laxative. It's a wonderful treat to the body if you want to get right with the Lord and if you want to start with your temple (the body). Taking the hyssop tea along with anointing yourself with hyssop oil is a great way to present yourself before the LORD.

FISH

I believe Jesus ate lots of fish, bread, and honey while on his journey to preach the good news throughout the Bible. Some scholars suggest that Jesus ate a lot of Tilapia and Perch. Some people believe based on the Levitical Laws that Catfish was a forbidden fish, so I do not believe Jesus ate Catfish. But what I do believe is that Jesus ate a lot of fish because remember he fed the 5000 with loaves of bread and fish. I believe Jesus stayed healthy because he did a lot of walking, drank plenty of water, ate bread, fish, and honey.

IN CONCLUSION

- Please drink plenty of water, and drink plenty of milk for your vitamin D. Why take a vitamin D pill when you can drink milk.

- Why take an iron pill when you can eat lots of spinach for your iron.

- Eat a little honey with your fresh lemon water to make lemonade. Choose healthy choices.

- Eat figs to increase your daily fiber and eat Post Raisin Bran to relieve constipation.

Dear friends, if you can, drink at least half of a gallon or more of water each day. Water will help pull out all pharmaceutical medicines stored in your bloodstream for months at a time. Water is power. Drink water, take baths with water, shower with water. Always keep water running inside of you or upon you. Water is a natural healing agent and is symbolic of the wells of Living Water and the Holy Spirit.

CHAPTER 6

25 HEALING SCRIPTURES

Deuteronomy 8:3

<u>I believe I receive my healing in Jesus Name</u>
"And he humbled thee, and suffered thee to hunger, and fed thee with manna, which thou knewest not, neither did thy fathers know; that he might make thee know that man doth not live by bread only, but by every word that proceedeth out of the mouth of the Lord doth man live." Deuteronomy 8:3

<u>I will read this scripture out loud in Jesus Name</u>
"And he humbled thee, and suffered thee to hunger, and fed thee with manna, which thou knewest not, neither did thy fathers know; that he might make thee know that man doth not live by bread only, but by every word that proceedeth out of the mouth of the Lord doth man live." Deuteronomy 8:3

<u>I will study this scripture in Jesus Name</u>
"And he humbled thee, and suffered thee to hunger, and fed thee with manna, which thou knewest not, neither did thy fathers know; that he might make thee know that man doth not live by bread only, but

by every word that proceedeth out of the mouth of the Lord doth man live." Deuteronomy 8:3

<u>I will write this scripture on paper in Jesus Name</u>
"And he humbled thee, and suffered thee to hunger, and fed thee with manna, which thou knewest not, neither did thy fathers know; that he might make thee know that man doth not live by bread only, but by every word that proceedeth out of the mouth of the Lord doth man live." Deuteronomy 8:3.

NOTES

WEEK: _____

HEALING SCRIPTURES

2 Chronicles 16:12

I believe I receive my healing in Jesus Name
"And Asa in the thirty and ninth year of his reign was diseased in his feet, until his disease was exceeding great: yet in his disease he sought not to the Lord, but to the physicians." 2 Chronicles 16:12

I will read this scripture out loud in Jesus Name
"And Asa in the thirty and ninth year of his reign was diseased in his feet, until his disease was exceeding great: yet in his disease he sought not to the Lord, but to the physicians." 2 Chronicles 16:12

I will study this scripture in Jesus Name
"And Asa in the thirty and ninth year of his reign was diseased in his feet, until his disease was exceeding great: yet in his disease he sought not to the Lord, but to the physicians." 2 Chronicles 16:12

I will write this scripture on paper in Jesus Name
"And Asa in the thirty and ninth year of his reign was diseased in his feet, until his disease was exceeding great: yet in his disease he sought not to the Lord, but to the physicians." 2 Chronicles 16:12

NOTES

WEEK: _____

HEALING SCRIPTURES

Job 13:4

I believe I receive my healing in Jesus Name
"But ye are forgers of lies; ye are all physicians of no value." Job 13:4

I will read this scripture out loud in Jesus Name
"But ye are forgers of lies; ye are all physicians of no value." Job 13:4

I will study this scripture in Jesus Name
"But ye are forgers of lies; ye are all physicians of no value." Job 13:4

I will write this scripture on paper in Jesus Name
"But ye are forgers of lies; ye are all physicians of no value." Job 13:4

NOTES

WEEK: _____

HEALING SCRIPTURES

Psalms 103:3

<u>I believe I receive my healing in Jesus Name</u>
"Bless the Lord, O my soul, and all that is within me bless his holy name. Bless the Lord O my soul and forget not all his benefits: Who forgiveth all thine iniquities, who healeth all thy diseases." Psalms 103:3

<u>I will read this scripture out loud in Jesus Name</u>
"Bless the Lord, O my soul, and all that is within me bless his holy name. Bless the Lord O my soul and forget not all his benefits: Who forgiveth all thine iniquities, who healeth all thy diseases." Psalms 103:3

<u>I will study this scripture in Jesus Name</u>
"Bless the Lord, O my soul, and all that is within me bless his holy name. Bless the Lord O my soul and forget not all his benefits: Who forgiveth all thine iniquities, who healeth all thy diseases." Psalms 103:3

<u>I will write this scripture on paper in Jesus Name</u>
"Bless the Lord, O my soul, and all that is within me bless his holy name. ...Psalms 103:3

NOTES

WEEK: _____

HEALING SCRIPTURES

Jeremiah 30:17

<u>I believe I receive my healing in Jesus Name</u>
"For I will restore health unto thee, and I will heal thee of thy wounds, saith the Lord." Jeremiah 30:17

<u>I will read this scripture out loud in Jesus Name</u>
"For I will restore health unto thee, and I will heal thee of thy wounds, saith the Lord." Jeremiah 30:17

<u>I will study this scripture in Jesus Name</u>
"For I will restore health unto thee, and I will heal thee of thy wounds, saith the Lord." Jeremiah 30:17

<u>I will write this scripture on paper in Jesus Name</u>
"For I will restore health unto thee, and I will heal thee of thy wounds, saith the Lord." Jeremiah 30:17

NOTES

WEEK: _____

HEALING SCRIPTURES

James 5:14-15

<u>I believe I receive my healing in Jesus Name</u>
"Is any sick among you? Let him call for the elders of the church; ***and let them pray over him***, anointing him with oil in the name of the Lord: And the prayer of faith shall save the sick, and the Lord shall raise him up." James 5:14-15.

<u>I will read this scripture out loud in Jesus Name</u>
"Is any sick among you? Let him call for the elders of the church; ***and let them pray over him***, anointing him with oil in the name of the Lord: And the prayer of faith shall save the sick, and the Lord shall raise him up." James 5:14-15.

<u>I will study this scripture in Jesus Name</u>
"Is any sick among you? Let him call for the elders of the church; ***and let them pray over him***, anointing him with oil in the name of the Lord: And the prayer of faith shall save the sick, and the Lord shall raise him up." James 5:14-15.

<u>I will write this scripture on paper in Jesus Name</u>
"Is any sick among you? Let him call for ....

NOTES

WEEK: _____

HEALING SCRIPTURES

Jeremiah 7:14

<u>I believe I receive my healing in Jesus Name</u>
"Heal me, O Lord, and I shall be healed; save me, and I shall be saved: for thou art my praise. Behold, they say unto me: Where is the word of the Lord? Let it come now." Jeremiah 17:14

<u>I will read this scripture out loud in Jesus Name</u>
"Heal me, O Lord, and I shall be healed; save me, and I shall be saved: for thou art my praise. Behold, they say unto me: Where is the word of the Lord? Let it come now." Jeremiah 17:14

<u>I will study this scripture in Jesus Name</u>
"Heal me, O Lord, and I shall be healed; save me, and I shall be saved: for thou art my praise. Behold, they say unto me: Where is the word of the Lord? Let it come now." Jeremiah 17:14

<u>I will write this scripture on paper in Jesus Name</u>
"Heal me, O Lord, and I shall be healed; save me, and I shall be saved: for thou art my praise. Behold, they say unto me; Where is the word of the Lord? Let it come now." Jeremiah 17:14

NOTES

WEEK: _____

HEALING SCRIPTURES

Isaiah 54:17

<u>I believe I receive my healing in Jesus Name</u>
"No weapon that is formed against thee shall prosper: and every tongue that shall rise against thee in judgment thou shalt condemn: This is the heritage of the servants of the Lord." Isaiah 54:17

<u>I will read this scripture out loud in Jesus Name</u>
"No weapon that is formed against thee shall prosper: and every tongue that shall rise against thee in judgment thou shalt condemn: This is the heritage of the servants of the Lord." Isaiah 54:17

<u>I will study this scripture in Jesus Name</u>
"No weapon that is formed against thee shall prosper: and every tongue that shall rise against thee in judgment thou shalt condemn: This is the heritage of the servants of the Lord." Isaiah 54:17

<u>I will write this scripture on paper in Jesus Name</u>
"No weapon that is formed against thee shall prosper: and every tongue that shall rise against thee in judgment thou shalt condemn…" Isaiah 54:17.

NOTES

WEEK: _____

HEALING SCRIPTURES

Psalms 107:20

<u>I believe I receive my healing in Jesus Name</u>
"He sent his word, and healed them, and delivered them from their destruction. Oh, that men would praise the Lord for his goodness." Psalms 107:20

<u>I will read this scripture out loud in Jesus Name</u>
"He sent his word, and healed them, and delivered them from their destruction. Oh, that men would praise the Lord for his goodness." Psalms 107:20

<u>I will study this scripture in Jesus Name</u>
"He sent his word, and healed them, and delivered them from their destruction. Oh, that men would praise the Lord for his goodness." Psalms 107:20

<u>I will write this scripture on paper in Jesus Name</u>
"He sent his word, and healed them, and delivered them from their destruction. Oh, that men would praise the Lord for his goodness. " Psalms 107:20

NOTES

WEEK: _____

HEALING SCRIPTURES

Isaiah 53:5

I believe I receive my healing in Jesus Name
"But he was wounded for our transgressions, he was bruised for our iniquities, the chastisement of our peace was upon him, and with his stripes we are healed."

I will read this scripture out loud in Jesus Name
"But he was wounded for our transgressions, he was bruised for our iniquities, the chastisement of our peace was upon him, and with his stripes we are healed."

I will study this scripture in Jesus Name
"But he was wounded for our transgressions, he was bruised for our iniquities, the chastisement of our peace was upon him, and with his stripes we are healed."

I will write this scripture on paper in Jesus Name
"But he was wounded for our transgressions, he was bruised for our iniquities, the chastisement of our peace was upon him, and with his stripes we are healed."

NOTES

WEEK: _____

HEALING SCRIPTURES

1 Peter 2:24

<u>I believe I receive my healing in Jesus Name</u>
"Who his own self bare our sins in his own body on the tree that we, being dead to sins, should live unto righteousness: by whose stripes ye were healed." 1Peter 2:24

<u>I will read this scripture out loud in Jesus Name</u>
"Who his own self bare our sins in his own body on the tree that we, being dead to sins, should live unto righteousness: by whose stripes ye were healed." 1Peter 2:24

<u>I will study this scripture in Jesus Name</u>
"Who his own self bare our sins in his own body on the tree that we, being dead to sins, should live unto righteousness: by whose stripes ye were healed." 1Peter 2:24

<u>I will write this scripture on paper in Jesus Name</u>
"Who his own self bare our sins in his own body on the tree that we, being dead to sins, should live unto righteousness: by whose stripes…1Peter 2:24

NOTES

WEEK: _____

HEALING SCRIPTURES

Matthew 10:1

<u>I believe I receive my healing in Jesus Name</u>
"And when he had called unto him his twelve disciples, he gave them power against unclean spirits, to cast them out, and to heal all manner of sickness and all manner of disease." Matthew 10:1

<u>I will read this scripture out loud in Jesus Name</u>
"And when he had called unto him his twelve disciples, he gave them power against unclean spirits, to cast them out, and to heal all manner of sickness and all manner of disease. "Matthew 10:1

<u>I will study this scripture in Jesus Name</u>
"And when he had called unto him his twelve disciples, he gave them power against unclean spirits, to cast them out, and to heal all manner of sickness and all manner of disease." Matthew 10:1

<u>I will write this scripture on paper in Jesus Name</u>
"And when he had called unto him his twelve disciples, he gave them power against unclean spirits, to cast them out, and to heal all manner of sickness and all manner of disease." Matthew 10:1

NOTES

WEEK:

HEALING SCRIPTURES

Psalms 41:3

<u>I believe I receive my healing in Jesus Name</u>
"The LORD will strengthen him upon the bed of languishing: thou wilt make all his bed in his sickness." Psalms 41:3

<u>I will read this scripture out loud in Jesus Name</u>
"The LORD will strengthen him upon the bed of languishing: thou wilt make all his bed in his sickness." Psalms 41:3

<u>I will study this scripture in Jesus Name</u>
"The LORD will strengthen him upon the bed of languishing: thou wilt make all his bed in his sickness." Psalms 41:3

<u>I will write this scripture on paper in Jesus Name</u>
"The LORD will strengthen him upon the bed of languishing: thou wilt make all his bed in his sickness." Psalms 41:3

NOTES

WEEK: _____

HEALING SCRIPTURES

Mark 16:16

<u>I believe I receive my healing in Jesus Name</u>
"And these signs shall follow them that believe. In my name they shall cast out devils; they shall speak with new tongues; they shall take up serpents; and if they drink any deadly thing it shall not hurt them; they shall lay hands on the sick and they shall recover." Mark 16:16

<u>I will read this scripture out loud in Jesus Name</u>
"And these signs shall follow them that believe. In my name they shall cast out devils; they shall speak with new tongues; they shall take up serpents; and if they drink any deadly thing it shall not hurt them; they shall lay hands on the sick and they shall recover." Mark 16:16

<u>I will study this scripture in Jesus Name</u>
"And these signs shall follow them that believe. In my name they shall cast out devils; they shall speak with new tongues; they shall take up serpents; and if they drink any deadly thing it shall not hurt them; they shall lay hands on the sick and they shall recover." Mark 16:16

<u>I will write this scripture on paper in Jesus Name…</u>

NOTES

WEEK: _____

HEALING SCRIPTURES

Isaiah 58:6-8

<u>I believe I receive my healing in Jesus Name</u>
"Is not this the fast that I have chosen?... Is it not to deal thy bread to the hungry…and when thou see the naked, cover him? Then shall thy light break forth as the morning, and thine health shall spring forth speedily." Isaiah 58:6-8

<u>I will read this scripture out loud in Jesus Name</u>
"Is not this the fast that I have chosen?... Is it not to deal thy bread to the hungry…and when thou see the naked, cover him? Then shall thy light break forth as the morning, and thine health shall spring forth speedily." Isaiah 58:6-8

<u>I will study this scripture in Jesus Name</u>
"Is not this the fast that I have chosen?... Is it not to deal thy bread to the hungry…and when thou see the naked, cover him? Then shall thy light break forth as the morning, and thine health shall spring forth speedily." Isaiah 58:6-8

<u>I will write this scripture on paper in Jesus Name</u>
"Is not this the fast that I have chosen?... Is it not to deal thy bread to the hungry…" Isaiah 58:6-8

NOTES

WEEK: _____

HEALING SCRIPTURES

Luke 9:11

<u>I believe I receive my healing in Jesus Name</u>
"And the people, when they knew it, followed him; and he received them, and spake unto them of the kingdom of God, and healed them that had need of healing." Luke 9:11

<u>I will read this scripture out loud in Jesus Name</u>
"And the people, when they knew it, followed him; and he received them, and spake unto them of the kingdom of God, and healed them that had need of healing." Luke 9:11

<u>I will study this scripture in Jesus Name</u>
"And the people, when they knew it, followed him; and he received them, and spake unto them of the kingdom of God, and healed them that had need of healing." Luke 9:11

<u>I will write this scripture on paper in Jesus Name</u>
"And the people, when they knew it, followed him; and he received them, and spake unto them of the kingdom of God, and healed them..." Luke 9:11

NOTES

WEEK: _____

HEALING SCRIPTURES

Acts 10:38

<u>I believe I receive my healing in Jesus Name</u>
"How God anointed Jesus of Nazareth with the Holy Ghost and with power: who went about doing good, and healing all that were oppressed of the devil: for God was with him." Acts 10:38

<u>I will read this scripture out loud in Jesus Name</u>
"How God anointed Jesus of Nazareth with the Holy Ghost and with power: who went about doing good, and healing all that were oppressed of the devil: for God was with him." Acts 10:38

<u>I will study this scripture in Jesus Name</u>
"How God anointed Jesus of Nazareth with the Holy Ghost and with power: who went about doing good, and healing all that were oppressed of the devil: for God was with him." Acts 10:38

<u>I will write this scripture on paper in Jesus Name</u>
"How God anointed Jesus of Nazareth with the Holy Ghost and with power: who went about doing good, and healing all that were oppressed of the devil: for God was with him." Acts 10:38

NOTES

WEEK: _____

HEALING SCRIPTURES

2 Kings 20:5

<u>I believe I receive my healing in Jesus Name</u>
"Thus saith the Lord, the God of David thy father, I have heard thy prayer, I have seen thy tears: behold, I will heal thee." 2 Kings 20:5

<u>I will read this scripture out loud in Jesus Name</u>
"Thus saith the Lord, the God of David thy father, I have heard thy prayer, I have seen thy tears: behold, I will heal thee." 2 King 20:5

<u>I will study this scripture in Jesus Name</u>
"Thus saith the Lord, the God of David thy father, I have heard thy prayer, I have seen thy tears: behold, I will heal thee." 2 King 20:5

<u>I will write this scripture on paper in Jesus Name</u>
"Thus saith the Lord, the God of David thy father, I have heard thy prayer, I have seen thy tears: behold, I will heal thee." 2 Kings 20:5

NOTES

WEEK: _____

HEALING SCRIPTURES

Deuteronomy 32:39

<u>I believe I receive my healing in Jesus Name</u>
"See now that I, even I, am he, and there is no god with me: I kill, and I make alive: I wound, and I heal: neither is there any that can deliver out of my hand." Deuteronomy 32:39

<u>I will read this scripture out loud in Jesus Name</u>
"See now that I, even I, am he, and there is no god with me: I kill, and I make alive: I wound, and I heal: neither is there any that can deliver out of my hand." Deuteronomy 32:39

<u>I will study this scripture in Jesus Name</u>
"See now that I, even I, am he, and there is no god with me: I kill, and I make alive: I wound, and I heal: neither is there any that can deliver out of my hand." Deuteronomy 32:39

<u>I will write this scripture on paper in Jesus Name</u>
"See now that I, even I, am he, and there is no god with me..." Deuteronomy 32:39

NOTES

WEEK: _____

HEALING SCRIPTURES

Hosea 14:4

<u>I believe I receive my healing in Jesus Name</u>
"I will heal their backsliding; I will love them freely; for mine anger is turned away from him." Hosea 14:4

<u>I will read this scripture out loud in Jesus Name</u>
"I will heal their backsliding; I will love them freely; for mine anger is turned away from him." Hosea 14:4

<u>I will study this scripture in Jesus Name</u>
"I will heal their backsliding; I will love them freely; for mine anger is turned away from him." Hosea 14:4

<u>I will write this scripture on paper in Jesus Name</u>
"I will heal their backsliding; I will love them freely; for mine anger is turned away from him." Hosea 14:4

NOTES

WEEK: _____

HEALING SCRIPTURES

Revelation 22:2

I believe I receive my healing in Jesus Name
"In the midst of the street of it, and on either side of the river, was there the tree of life, which bare twelve manners of fruits, and yielded her fruit every month: and the leaves of the tree were for the healing of the nations." Revelation 22:2

I will read this scripture out loud in Jesus Name
"In the midst of the street of it, and on either side of the river, was there the tree of life, which bare twelve manners of fruits, and yielded her fruit every month: and the leaves of the tree were for the healing of the nations." Revelation 22:2

I will study this scripture in Jesus Name
"In the midst of the street of it, and on either side of the river, was there the tree of life, which bare twelve manners of fruits, and yielded her fruit every month: and the leaves of the tree were for the healing of the nations." Revelation 22:2

I will write this scripture on paper in Jesus Name
"In the midst of the street of it…" Revelation 22:2

NOTES

WEEK: _____

HEALING SCRIPTURES

Luke 8:43-48

<u>I believe I receive my healing in Jesus Name</u>
"And a woman having an issue of blood twelve years, which had spent all her living upon physicians, neither could be healed of any, Came behind him, and touched the border of his garment: and immediately her issue of blood stanched.

And Jesus said, Who touched me? When all denied, Peter and they that were with him said, Master, the multitude throng thee and press thee, and sayest thou, Who touched me?

And Jesus said, Somebody hath touched me: for I perceive that virtue is gone out of me. And when the woman saw that she was not hid, she came trembling, and falling down before him, she declared unto him before all the people for what cause she had touched him, and how she was healed immediately.

And he said unto her, Daughter, be of good comfort: thy faith hath made thee whole; go in peace. Luke 8:43-48

NOTES

WEEK: _____

HEALING SCRIPTURES

Malachi 4:2

<u>I believe I receive my healing in Jesus Name</u>
"But unto you that fear my name shall the Sun of righteousness arise with healing in his wings." Malachi 4:2

<u>I will read this scripture out loud in Jesus Name</u>
"But unto you that fear my name shall the Sun of righteousness arise with healing in his wings." Malachi 4:2

<u>I will study this scripture in Jesus Name</u>
"But unto you that fear my name shall the Sun of righteousness arise with healing in his wings." Malachi 4:2

<u>I will write this scripture on paper in Jesus Name</u>
"But unto you that fear my name shall the Sun of righteousness arise with healing in his wings." Malachi 4:2

NOTES

WEEK: _____

HEALING SCRIPTURES

Psalm 34:19

<u>I believe I receive my healing in Jesus Name</u>
"Many are the afflictions of the righteous: but the Lord delivereth him out of them all." Psalm 34:19

<u>I will read this scripture out loud in Jesus Name</u>
"Many are the afflictions of the righteous: but the Lord delivereth him out of them all." Psalm 34:19

<u>I will study this scripture in Jesus Name</u>
"Many are the afflictions of the righteous: but the Lord delivereth him out of them all." Psalm 34:19

<u>I will write this scripture on paper in Jesus Name</u>
"Many are the afflictions of the righteous: but the Lord delivereth him out of them all." Psalm 34:19

NOTES

WEEK: _____

HEALING SCRIPTURES

Jeremiah 33:6

<u>I believe I receive my healing in Jesus Name</u>
"Behold, I will bring it health and cure, and I will cure them, and will reveal unto them the abundance of peace and truth." Jeremiah 33:6

<u>I will read this scripture out loud in Jesus Name</u>
"Behold, I will bring it health and cure, and I will cure them, and will reveal unto them the abundance of peace and truth." Jeremiah 33:6

<u>I will study this scripture in Jesus Name</u>
"Behold, I will bring it health and cure, and I will cure them, and will reveal unto them the abundance of peace and truth." Jeremiah 33:6

<u>I will write this scripture on paper in Jesus Name</u>
"Behold, I will bring it health and cure, and I will cure them, and will reveal unto them the abundance of peace and truth." Jeremiah 33:6

NOTES

WEEK: _____

PRAYER TO RECEIVE ETERNAL LIFE

Dear Heavenly Father, I invite you in my heart to be my Lord and Saviour. I pray dear Lord that I may become a brand-new creature by way of the preaching of the Gospel. I pray that your Spirit will draw me to the waters of baptism so that I may repent and be baptized and receive the gift of the Holy Ghost, according to Acts 2:38 KJV Bible. Take away those things in my life that are associated with ungodly pleasures. I choose to obey you by giving up old habits such as smoking or drinking so that my light will shine and that I may glorify the Father which art in heaven.

Thank you for the prayers that my parents and grandparents and other saints from the Church have prayed on my behalf. Thank you for being faithful to me, Heavenly Father. Because of the fact I am reading this book I know that the Almighty God is leading and guiding my path in Jesus Name.

DAILY PRAYER CONFESSION FOR THE BELIEVER

"I am the body of Christ, so Satan has no power over me, and I overcome evil with good." (1 Corinthians 12:27: Romans 12:21)

"No weapon formed against me shall prosper, for my righteousness is of (from) the Lord. But whatever I do will prosper for I'm like a tree that's planted by the rivers of water." (Isaiah 54:17:Psalm 1:3)

"My God will meet all my needs according to His riches in glory in Christ Jesus." (Philippians 4:19)

"I am of (from) God and have overcome Satan, because the one who is in me is greater than the one who is in the world." (1 John 4:4)

"I will fear no evil, for you are with me, Lord; Your Word and Your Staff they comfort me." (Psalm 23:4)

"I am far from oppression, and fear does not come near me." (Isaiah 54:14)

Quotes By Charles Capps

ABOUT THE AUTHOR

Aletha Rena Doggett is a born-again believer following the principles and ways of the Most High God, Jesus Christ. Aletha received a prophecy from Apostle Richard D. Henton in 2004 that she had a lot of gifts and talents and was a leader who needed to come to the front. Aletha discovered that she was a minister and seer of the gospel, a writer, and a publisher. Aletha has written several books and has launched her own publishing company – ARD Book Services. Aletha was born in Detroit, Michigan, and is the youngest of 7 siblings. Aletha is single, loves to bake cakes, pies, and desires to be married and have her own family.

Books by Aletha Rena Doggett

Alhaji and the Sunshine Kids
Lord, Please Send Me My Husband
Be Healed and Stay Healed in Jesus Name
Is Diabetes a Principality?
100 Questions you should ask before Marriage

ARD Book Services
www.ardbookservices.com

ARD Book Services

Made in the USA
Columbia, SC
25 September 2024

42367719R00059